The Keys of Change

CREATE
AND
ORCHESTRATE
YOUR FUTURE

robboverholt

Yellowdoor
PRESS Austin, TX

THE KEYS OF CHANGE

ISBN: 0692368795
ISBN-13: 978-0692368794

First edition 2015
Printed in the United States of America

Yellow Door Press
For bulk orders, permission requests, and other inquiries, email
info@robboverholt.com

Cover design: Tyler Downing
Interior design: Dene Shelding

FOR HER

My bride, my partner, and the greatest supporter of my work in this world. Thank you, Shaula, this book would simply not exist without your support. I'm so glad that you're still holding on. I love you like mad.

FOR THEM

My son, Logan, a warrior-poet, and my daughter, Laney, a warrior-princess…
I hope both of you have gained half as much from me as I have profited from you. Words fail to convey how proud of you I am and how very much I love you both.

CONTENTS

ACKNOWLEDGMENTS

I would like to thank just a few people who have not only shaped my thinking, but have challenged me to always grow, which is the very essence of change. Some have done this in close proximity, while others' influence has been felt from afar.

Ben Arment. Mike Rayburn.
Erwin Raphael McManus.
Eric Michael Bryant.
Philip Yancey. Lori Overholt.
Ron Jones. P. David Hewson.
Paul King. R. Guill.
Thanks to each of you for pushing me to always be a better version of myself.

FOREWORD

At the recommendation of a common friend Robb Overholt and I met for breakfast at the Sunrise Cafe in Las Vegas, a new home for both of our families. After talking for a few minutes, the unfolding chain of, "Hold it, so you're the guy they said...?" and "Oh, you mean you know him, too?" and "They told me who you were..." was remarkable - a "God-kind-of-thing," indeed.

Whatever the circumstance, meet we did and I say with all humility, I am a better human being for it. I have worked, performed and served with Robb Overholt for the better part of a decade and I can tell you, his depth of wisdom and life experience is rivaled only by his artistic ability to share that wisdom.

And hence, this book, "The Keys of Change!"

What you are about to experience is the result of years of hard work, struggle, learning, and finally… triumph. Every time I hear Robb speak it's a breath of fresh air. In "The Keys of Change" Robb has managed to capture the essence of his keynote presentations in written form, which is no easy task.

Robb's stories are engaging in and of themselves, so much so you barely notice that you're learning something. When he then draws from them a timeless life lesson, one anyone can apply immediately for immeasurable benefit, it's just beautiful.

I suggest you read this book with your "success journal" - a composition book or spiral notebook - close by for two reasons. First, you'll want to take notes on what you read. More importantly and in addition, you'll want to record your *own* thoughts; the personal ideas and revelations this book inspires in *you*. You see, that's what Robb Overholt and his "The Keys Of Change" are really all about; not just impressing you with his art and wisdom, but inspiring you to transform, to become a higher vision of yourself.

And that is a "God-kind-of-thing," too.
Enjoy.

- Mike Rayburn

robboverholt

4

TWO WEEKS

Monday, March 19th, 2012 - 9:18am CST:

My wife and I, with the wind in our sails, are in full anticipation of our long-planned family vacation to Key West that we depart for in just two days. It's been a hard six weeks as my wife is still in recovery from a recent surgery, and the Doc has given her permission to travel just in the nick of t me. We are anxious to get away with our children for a little, much-needed rest and relaxation. It's all the two of us can talk about as we step into the company offices in Chicagoland, where we are both employed with the same consulting firm. My dream job. One that I'd spent the last twenty years working towards. One that I plan to work in for the next twenty years before sailing off into the sunset of retirement.

Our Monday morning meeting with the COO begins abruptly. We are immediately informed that the company is bleeding out financially. We are told finances have been in critical condition even since before we were brought on to start a new division in what had been an ingenious new conglomerate scenario (or so we thought). We sit, wondering why we were hired on (just a year ago) to work on a start-up (with its necessary expenditures) while the company was obviously in dire straits. It is in that moment that we are informed that our division and all of its funding are being cut effective immediately. We are being "let go" (as if it were a privilege). No severance package. No options. Next paycheck, due in just 11 days, will be our very last. What we don't yet know is that the company as a whole will only survive a few more months after our departure. Knowing that would not have made us feel any better at the time. We leave the office, stunned, with the wind knocked out of us, vacation now the furthest thing from our mind... at least the rest and relaxation part of it.

2 Weeks later
Monday, April 2nd, 2012 - 11:39am CST:

I'm sitting on the sofa in our family room, recovering from a not-so-relaxing time away in Florida (after all, the vacation had already been paid for). As I comb through my mind, I can't help but wonder how we could use that money now though. The "If only I had..." and the "Why didn't I..." refrains are racing through my brain like a bullet train. I am diligently attempting to stave off the trappings of "Poor Me."

As a family, we are already busy making arrangements and preparing for our second major move in consecutive years when my phone rings. It's our realtor in Las Vegas. We still own a home there that's been on the real-estate market (that has crashed) for well over a year now. He asks me a simple question that I'll never forget...

"Hey Robb, did you rent out the house?"

"No... You're our realtor. You'd know if we did. Hey, wait a second, why are you asking me that?"

Long pause.
"Well, I guess we have a problem..."

I guess we have a problem indeed. "Squatters," as they are called, have taken possession of our home in Las Vegas at this point. Busted open the Lock Box and stolen the key. Changed the locks and moved in as if it were their dream home. Because of antiquated laws on the books of Nevada, and several other ridiculous things that I'll refrain from mentioning here, it will take us over a year to get them evicted from our home. A home where they do not have a legal lease and have stolen possession of a property that we are responsible for. During their fifteen month, rent-free stay, they will wreak havoc on the property, and leave it in utter wreckage upon their exit.

Two Weeks in the Spring of 2012. Those two weeks would dramatically change our lives. The type of change we weren't looking for and we would certainly not welcome. I have since compared those two weeks to the feeling of moseying a ong when someone suddenly opens a trap door. It was and still, at times, continues to seem… Surreal.

Since the days of that Spring, I have spent the bulk of my time writing, crafting, and honing the material that you now hold in your hands. I have practiced the action-plan that this book contains. It's relatively brief and makes for an easy, engaging read. It's simple, but don't let that fool you… There is a power in its simplicity. My background as a musician bleeds all over it. You'll be glad, as the music-based metaphors keep things engaging while syncing up to practical strategies for positive outcomes, regardless of what's being thrown at you. These principles have worked for me and they will work for anyone, in any walk of life, in any career, always... Because they are time tested.

It's not as if I'm alone in this journey. I'm not the only one who has ever lost a job. Even a dream job. I'm not the only one who has ever had his credit severely damaged in a bad housing market. Fact is, I'm not even the only one who has had his home stolen and his finances devastated by a band of thieves known as "squatters." I'm in a serious minority on that last one, but I'm still not the *only* one. And I'm certainly not the only one who has ever lost *someone* even more valuable than anything I've already mentioned. It's true; I'm not the first person, and I won't be the last, who had plans, only to see those plans wrecked by a sudden, un-welcomed Change.

Social Science informs us that 75 percent of the general population suffers at least "some stress" - due to transitions and change - every, (wouldn't you know it?), *two weeks*. Half of those experience moderate or high levels during the same period (according to the National Health Interview Survey). Unwillingness to manage this stress is a contributing factor in many health issues and decreased productivity. Furthermore, those who cope well with transitions and change have a more positive perception, a better quality of life, and a higher level of performance at work and at play.

The theme of this book, of course, is change. But not from the lens of a cynic, I promise you. It's not filled with naivety and fluff either. I understand full well, that change can be difficult. But you see, I've never thought, nor will I ever be inclined to think that change is the enemy. Change is a natural, wonderful, mysterious, and necessary agent of growth. I appreciate it as such. After all, I don't want to be the same person I was when I was three years old, right?

I am now more passionate than ever about helping everyone understand that change need not limit us, and it can often propel us forward in all the best ways. It's for these reasons that I now travel with this material and speak everywhere I can about it. It is simply something that I LOVE to do, and wouldn't be doing, had it not been for the sake of change. But in order to see this truth, I had to be willing to look back. If I was going to continue to create my future, I had to start by remembering something simple, but very important, from my past. That's where we are heading off to now.

A WALK IN THE PARK

So there I am, not even yet a year removed from high school. I am on my way into a theme park with a group of friends for a day of fun. Now, I should inform you that one of these friends is a girl — who has... well, struck my fancy. I am quite smitten with her, as it were. And this day to which I refer is going to be a great day because I am going to get to spend it with her. In fact, I am secretly hoping to make my affections known to her on this very day. I just have no idea at this point, and it never (in a million years) would occur to me, just how that is about to happen.

So, we're entering the park when all the girls in the crew immediately head off to the bathroom together. I know, cliche - but true. I'm standing with a couple of the guys waiting for the girls to reappear. One of my friends, we'll call him Bobby (because, well, that is actually his name and he's not on the run or anything, so I think it's ok)... Bobby says something to me that immediately causes my heart to accelerate.

Bobby: "I think I'm going to go for it today with..." (and then says the name of the girl whom I am telling you about right now).

I immediately (heart now in my throat) turn and blurt out: "NO! Uh, you know, um, I'm just saying, uh, no, you... you can't do that."

Bobby (puzzled): "Why not?"

Sweat is now beading up on my brow, and I just stare at him with a blank look for a few seconds that feel like forever.

And then a curious look comes over his face as he asks, "Oh... Is something going on between the two of you?"

Like he has just given me a gift, I exclaim: "Uh... Yeah! Yep, that's it! Man, you figured it out. So, ya know... sorry."

Bobby: "You guys are together?!" (Like it's almost too hard to believe).

Me (slightly annoyed): "Yes!"

Bobby: "Is this a new thing?"

Me: "Yeah, pretty new. It's... it's brand new."

Bobby: "How did I not know? Does anybody else know?"

Me: "Nope. Nobody knows. You are, (literally), the first to find out. It's, um, you know, still kind of a low key kind of thing. We... we just want to be sure that there's really something there before we make a big fuss about it." (I honestly don't know how I pulled that one off). "So, you know, don't say anything... to ANYBODY."

Bobby: "Oh, yeah... smart. Wow! Man, I'm sorry; I had no idea. But your secret's totally safe with me."

But I know better. It is only a matter of time before the word will be out, and I'll be outed to the world. And I will be the laughing-stock. With that thought fresh in my mind, the girls are now making their way out of the bathroom, and they are heading straight towards us.

And there she is, radiant, brown hair blowing in the breeze... Sporting those Reebok sneakers. Oh yeah. I know what I have to do. So I walk right up to this girl who is now right in the middle of the pack... I look her right in the face and belt out a serenade for her at the top of my lungs... *Boasting proudly of my heroic intentions and the power of my kisses to ease her pain* as if I were Enrique Iglesias himself.

Ok, that's not what happened at all. But what did happen is almost just as good. I did walk up to her right there in front of everyone...

Me: "We need to talk. Um..." (nervous chuckle) "The um; the funniest thing just happened. I mean, whew... you are really gonna get a kick out of this."

Her: "Really? What?"

Me: "Well, some of us guys were just standing over there waiting for you girls, and... well, Bobby... you know Bobby? Um, he told me... well, he said he wanted to make a play for you today."

Her: "Really?! And... you're telling me this because?"

Me: "Well... I might have... Actually; I told him he couldn't do that."

Her: "Really?! And... why would you do that?"

Me: "Well, I sort of implied that you and I were already an item."

Her: "You did? And... why would you do *that*?"

Me: "Um..." (starting to smile now as I find myself picking up some confidence) "Well, because I was kind of hoping that's the way it could be."

And with that, I grab her by the hand, and I just start walking and taking her away from the others. All of these years later, I can still distinctly remember feeling incredibly vulnerable at that moment, thinking, "If she lets go of my hand or pulls hers away, it's over for me. I'll be the butt of every joke. But if she doesn't let go... well…"

Suddenly, like Neil Diamond before me, it was as if I could hear the familiar refrain of *hands coming into contact with other hands that were reaching out to touch someone* like an old AT&T commercial. Yes, I could even hear the trumpets blasting "bah, bah, bah" from the soundtrack of my mind, and you know what? *Seldom had good times ever seemed this good. I too had been inclined to think that they never could or would.* And as the song in my mind crescendoed, I realized…

She DIDN'T let go.
In fact, she held on… tight. And still is.

At the time of this writing, we are right in the middle of our twenty-second year of marriage. Her name is Shaula, and I don't regret for a second taking a chance that day and I wouldn't change a thing if I had it all to do again... Really. I've examined it from every angle in the years that have followed since, and I'd still do it, even if it had not worked out in my favor. Sure, a few people may have or would have snickered at me. But underneath it all, they would have admired my courage. I would have survived it. Even if it hadn't gone my way. Honestly, at least I would have known... So that my place "shall never be with those cold and timid souls who know neither victory nor defeat." - Be careful, I just spilled a little Teddy Roosevelt all over you.

The truth is, I just wanted to do something. Do you know what I mean? I wanted to be pro-active - To take charge of my circumstances and change my trajectory. I wanted to make something happen rather than waiting for something I didn't want to happen to happen to me. And, as a result, something interesting happened. I learned something valuable that day. I learned that life was going to keep moving forward whether I chose to participate in it or not. Someone was always going to get the girl. Someone was always going to get the sale. Procure the contract. Seal the deal. Someone was always going to get what I wanted. And it might as well be me. And the truth is, it could just as easily be you too. I learned that the people and things around me would continue to change. If I wanted to have a say in how it would all happen, I'd better, not only get involved, but I'd better start being intentional about making my imprint. And so should you.

I want you to know that I refuse to believe that people hate change. You hear that all the time, right? "Well, ya know... people hate change..." No, we don't. People love change. If it weren't so, the world would not progress and evolve as it has and does. Think about it, we can't wait to upgrade our smartphones. Yeah, we love change. The truth is; we just hate the change we can't control. We hate when things change, and we didn't get a say in it.

I'll give you an example: If you decide to change your career because you're burned out, spent, whatever... You love the change and embrace it even if it brings great challenges, and it will bring a slew of challenges. It could involve going back to school. It will, very likely, involve learning a new trade or mastering new skills. Then there's understanding a new work culture and starting anew with no tenure on the bottom rung of the social strata, etc. But you will meet these demands with a fervor and a firm belief that this is the best thing for you and your future. However… If your employer decides it's time for you to make a career change, well... You hate that change, am I right? And you will despise all the same challenges that you would have tackled with determination had it been something of your choosing.

Another example: You decide to move, because you've always dreamt of living on the coast, near your family, whatever. You need this, because you know you need to get a clean start. That being the case, you love and embrace the change with all of its impending challenges, and it will bring challenges. Houses to sell and purchase. Leases to negotiate. Leaving old friends. Making new ones. Learning a new ethos and culture in a new town. But you embrace each one of these challenges and face them head on. Now, if your mortgage holder or landlord or employer decides it's time for you to move? Well, you hate that change and resist the very same obstacles that you would have hurdled had it been your decision. You get it. And on and on and on it goes. It really is just a matter of perspective, isn't it?

We know that "change" itself is not inherently bad. Think about it, your boss comes to you and informs you that you are getting a pay raise of 20 thousand per year. You don't say, "Oh, no... I hate change! And that's going to change everything. I can't accept that!" No one would ever say that. If, by chance, you think you are the one person who would not be able to cope, just know that I'd be happy to take those 20 G's off your hands. That's just the kind of guy I am.

So what should we do? Well, we should create change, rather than waiting for it to happen to us. Seems obvious, right? And, yet, it's not that simple, and we don't want to change just for change sake. But, clearly, we need a healthier view of change and our desire to control it. The truth is, the only things we have a modicum of control over are ourselves and the choices that we make. Turns out, the only way to change "things" is to change you... And then you'll notice how things around you start to change too. And that must be true, because it rhymes. Go ahead, read it again. I'll wait.

You see, I have always believed in, but sometimes need to be reminded of, the power of one of our most incredible verbs with two very important meanings...

re·solve
/rəˈzälv/
verb
1. decide firmly on a course of action.
2. settle or find a solution to (a problem, dispute, or contentious matter).

The truth is, in order for me to survive those "Two Weeks in the Spring of 2012," (or anything else life might throw my way), I was going to have to resolutely do both.

Turning negative life events, be them potential or actual ones, into something positive is totally possible, but never accidental. This type of thing only comes as a result of great intentionality. People don't just happen to make their way into a positive change through difficult circumstances in their life, saying, "What? Huh? How did this happen? I don't know."

From here on out, I'm going to give you a clear path of intentionality. Because you are far more likely to get the outcomes you desire by pursuing the outcomes you desire. Yes, you read that correctly and, yes, it's just that simple. And this type of pro-activity, this resolve, will create positive "life change" for you... As an individual... As an organization... For your families, and everyone that you have contact with, regardless of what is being thrown at you.

We are going to look at the two, fundamental, Keys of Change. Understanding these keys will not only unleash your potential, it will also reveal the mystery of change, so that it is no longer something to be feared. These keys focus on two basic choices that you have, and you and your choices are the only things you have any real control over (in case you forgot what you just read like 45 seconds ago). Along with these keys, I'm also going to give you some critical tools and ask you some tough questions. All of this is so that you can orchestrate and affect, not to mention, cope with the effects of change in your life, both personally and professionally. These keys, when understood and orchestrated well, lead to a dam-burst of positive change, even if you are drowning in the midst of an un-welcomed one right this very minute.

THE KEY OF RISK
RISK LIKE A LOVE SONG

The First Key we're going to play in and with is: The Key of Risk.
I want you to Risk.
I want you to Risk well.
I want you "to decide firmly on a course of action."
I want you to **Risk Like a Love Song!**

I know. I know… Even youth starlets like Selena Gomez from the Mickey Mouse channel recognize that *we've all heard the beautiful refrains of love songs presented and sung over and over and over and over again.* But, *I guess, she'll bring forward yet another one in which she'll express her love by using a simile that is actually a love song.* From there, *she/we will keep hitting repeat, with heavy emphasis on peat,* ad nauseam as if we can't get enough. (If, by chance, you don't recognize the hints regarding this song, ask your kids, a niece, a nephew, a kid on the street, etc.) Additionally, we've all been reminded of this fact long before by one-half of the greatest song writing duo of all-time, none other than Paul McCartney. With his second band, the Wings, he told us that *as silly as love songs can be, some people were audacious enough to keep filling the earth with them... to which he could find no fault at all.* (Young people, if you do not recognize these hints, ask your parents. And shame on you.)

I just did a written-word mash-up of Selena Gomez and Sir Paul McCartney. Give me some props for that. Who would dare? The former hails from Waverly Place in the land of Disney where pop princesses are churned out like butter. The latter of which is an all-time great… A young lad from Liverpool, who famously walked the Abbey Road of Beatles fame. And, yet, they both seem to agree, from different generations, times, and places, that we've had an abundance of love songs. Paul McCartney penned his silly little lyric regarding love songs way back in 1976, nearly forty years ago, and it sounds like it could have been written *Yesterday*. (Some of you might actually appreciate just how clever that last sentence really is.)

Honestly, though, you'd think that the world would already have enough. There are a countless number of them already in existence. In fact, it is believed that love songs date back as far as 4000 BC. Sonnets, poems, and tunes expressed by one smitten lover to another throughout the entire known history of humanity. And while each generation can argue the quality, there is no debating that, to this very day, love songs have not diminished in quantity… And they don't seem to be going away any time in the near future.

6,000 years of love songs. Think about it. The crooning, the wailing, the "heart-on-the-sleeve" chorus cry to sing along to with lighters or cell phones lifted high. Time and time again, every generation needs them, because a longing in humanity is awoken by the vulnerability of a songster or a songstress who dares to risk with a resolve to do something great. Sure, it might be silly. And, on the surface, we may even make fun of them at times. But underneath it all, we all know that we really admire their courage.

So, as it turns out, the world has NOT had enough love songs. This is why I live by a little something I call:
The Love Song Code.

What's The Love Song Code, you ask? So glad that you did (even if you didn't). It's simple, really. It's asking yourself, "What is going to be the soundtrack of my life?" And, then applying the answer. You see, I believe all 6,000 years of love songs could be boiled down into one of two categories. Sure, there are many sub-plots, but basically, there are but two fundamental kinds of love songs.

One is about "Risk," and the other is about "Regret."
It's the "Wonderment, and Wide-Eyed View of the World through Risk" - or - the "Woe-is-Me, What does He/She Have that I Don't Have Blues of Regret."
"Inspiration" - or - "Frustration."
The sheer joy of "An Endless, Eternal Love" - or - the agony of "A Love that Stinks... and Bites and Stings even."
It's, essentially, "Do I want to create positive change in my life, regardless of any and all circumstances or odds, and leave an imprint on the World?" - or - "Do I want the World to leave its imprint on me?" (Which, coincidentally, looks an awful lot like a tread mark).

I call the first grouping **"Love Songs of Intent"** and the second, **"Love Songs of Lament."** And remember, there is no positive change that happens without intent.

So, as a thesis, first, let's consider a "Love Song of Intent." An unsuspected one at that. It's a throwback to the hair bands and their infectious ballads. One for the ages. One that can make the hardest of hearts malleable. I'm thinking of a particular song given to us by notorious skull and cross bone rockers that would welcome you into the jungle with an appetite for destructive behavior. Crafted by guys that are called things like Axl and Slash. Crooning as the singer expresses *his affections for a sweet object of desire with a child-like innocence that he is reminded of by her smile.* Proclaiming that *if he stares too long into her face, he finds it difficult to fight back tears.*

Do you think it was the tight pants that allowed him to hit those high notes, by the way? Honestly, it was just crazy...

But, really, think about it... *Not being able to withstand the thought of her having pain in her blue-sky eyes. he seeks shelter in the locks of her hair.* This is where he prays for the storms above to pass through without much fuss. That kind of stuff doesn't sound like what those gentlemen looked like. (It's as odd as pairing up Guns with Roses, I suppose). Seriously, though, that's radical stuff. That's vulnerability. It's head-and-heart out on sleeves, and I don't care who-knows-or-what-comes type of risk. And it's just so inspiring.

Consider the alternative.
I'm thinking of one for the hip-hop fans now…

Our songster, Nelly, is *thinking of her as he's thinking of himself. Thinking of the two of them and their potential as he awakens to realize it is all but a dream. He travels down a familiar road as he ponders whether she might come back to him or not, realizing, again that he's only dreaming. He had been number one in her life, but now he has been relegated to a basement dwelling. She has found someone else. Now he can't stand knowing someone else is with his baby as he realizes he should have done more* and possibly taken the advice of Beyonce and put *a ring* where it belonged. *It's so overwhelming, he feels it in the atmosphere* like he's Phil Collins. He's now begging for empathy from the listener, asking them to *raise their hands if they have ever loved someone like he has, knowing that it's too late.* It's not just some dream; it's an all-too-often nightmare reality that we can all understand.

It's the "Love Song of Lament" — with its bitter grief, its broken heart, and its nagging regret. I should have done more. Why didn't I do something when I still had the chance? These are bitter pills to swallow. Seriously, life is short, but it's the longest thing you'll ever do on earth. And it's even longer when you have to do it with regret.

Interestingly, (and please don't miss this) whereas fear may at times keep us from taking a risk (fear of the unknown, rejection, loss, pain, looking stupid or foolish, etc.), it seldom can spare us from feeling those very same things in the long run if we don't. For if we do nothing, we end up looking back, feeling uncertain, rejected, lost, hurt, and, often, stupid or foolish. Take a moment and really think about this paragraph. The fact is, the same fear that keeps us from being bold, will abandon us when we are not.

You may, at this point, be thinking, "I get it, Robb... I know what you're saying, get back up on the horse, try again. But I have already been through so much. If you only knew what I have been through, you'd understand my hesitation."
Would I? Should I? No. Don't settle.

I get to travel around and speak on this subject for a lot of different organizations in many different places in the market. I hear time and time again about things like the downturned economy and how everything has changed, personally and professionally. I've taken note that this has caused a lot of people (and a lot of companies) to clamp their fists in fear. I want to urge you to resist that reflex. Instead, open your hands to the potential possibility that these days might bring.

Be Bold. Not in some utopian, Pollyanna manner. But with the resolve of a determined grit to do something great when we all need something great to happen.

Let's speak practically. All good risk-analysis should begin with two basic steps. First, "Identify the Threats" and the probability of something going wrong. You should realize that these threats could come from any number of sources depending on your particular situation. Could be a competitor, rival, business partner, co-worker, family member, friend, foe, spouse, boss, a new law/policy, the government, you name it. Then, secondly, "Scale Out and Weigh the Potential Loss and Gains" as you consider the consequences of each. Always (and I mean, always) remember, not all threats are bad. And there are certainly times when the prospect of a loss is what propels us... Often more so than the potential gains. These type of threats are often what drives innovation and peak performance.

Remember Bobby (from A Walk in the Park)? He presented a real threat to me, and it helped me get bold and creative in a way that forged an optimum outcome that still drives me years later. It is conceivable to me that that very day might have come and gone without me ever making my affections and intentions known to my eventual bride if it weren't for Bobby and the threat he presented. In that moment (and in every moment since), the thought of him, or anyone else, being with Shaula, rather than me, was more than I could stand and it served as a necessary push.

So, with those thoughts fresh in your mind, I want you to consider a few questions before you move forward.

Professionally:
- As a company, in your business, in your job, what is it that you couldn't

stomach to watch your competitors beat you to the market with?

- What do you need to do to step up to the plate and how can you Risk Like a Love Song to make something positive happen rather than waiting for something you don't want to happen to happen to you?

- What position, promotion, potential in you remains untapped or unachieved? How can you, right now, create a positive change and Risk Like a Love Song to make it happen?

Personally:

- In your marriage or relationships, what do you need to do, right now to put your head and heart all in and... Risk Like a Love Song?

- What goal or dream, a "dare-to-be-great" type of thing, is lying dormant within you and you know that you need to reignite it and start taking some chances to see it realized? How can you Risk Like a Love Song, in spite of setbacks and/or negative circumstances, in order to begin to make it happen?

Re-prioritize your goals, even if you are in the midst of something difficult right now. Sometimes we allow ourselves to believe that the current challenge/difficulty precludes us from moving forward with our "dare-to-be-great" ambition. We use this type of thinking as our first and best excuse. It's simply not true.

So what's your "dare-to-be-great" thing? The thing randomly keeping you up at night? The thing that rears its head, with no regard for difficult circumstances, and makes you think, "You know what would be great, is if I could leverage this so that…" You know what it is… I know you do.

I want to challenge you. In the context of this challenge, I want to give you three simple instructions to follow in the pursuit of your "dare-to-be-great" thing. With each one, I will address the fear that accompanies it. Along with the fear, I will give you the truth that the fear muddies up and keeps us from seeing clearly. Don't listen to the fear. The fear will abandon you.

1. **Declare it.** Take the risk of saying it out loud... Tell somebody. Not everybody, but somebody.
   - *The Fear:* Accountability. You fear that someone will now check in with you and ask how things are going on your quest.   How do you know if you have this fear? You may surmise "This is no one else's business. This is personal." You may even say things (to yourself) like, "I don't really know anyone that I respect enough to speak into my life this way." These are lies you tell yourself to keep from dealing with the fear.
   - *The Truth:* Declaring your ambition will inspire you to take it seriously. It will inspire others to do the same. If someone should snicker, or think you silly, you should know that they really admire your courage. If they resist, it is only

because it leaves them without excuse for pursuing their own ambitions.

2. **Commit to it.** Risk writing it down... Over and over again.
   - *The Fear:* Commitment. There is within you a fear that if you put something down in writing it makes it real. Too real... Contractual. Writing it down removes plausible deniability. After all, if it's not in writing, you can simply deny that you ever said or thought it in the first place.
   - *The Truth:* Writing it down is the first stage of making a concrete plan. With a plan, you *can* move forward with your ambition. Without one, you remain stagnant. The only difference between you and those you deem successful at the thing you want is that they had the guts to push past this fear.

3. **Act on it.** Risk taking action. Even if it's the smallest increment.

- *The Fear:* Failure. There is a fear that if you take action and don't fully realize your ambition, you are worthless, and you'd rather not face up to that. This fear convinces you that inaction allows you to hold on to "the dream" and that this fantasy is better than an uncertain reality.

- *The Truth:* The real, dirty truth is that if you always settle for "do-able" things, do you know what you'll always get? "Do-able" things. But if you go for the GREAT thing... I admit, you may not always get it... But you'll certainly get a whole lot more than you would have if you had just settled for the "do-able." Living with regret will feel like a *real* failure later on. Go ahead and get started.

Think of it this way moving forward: "Love Songs of Intent" are for those who want to create positive change regardless of their circumstances or odds. "Love Songs of Lament" are for those who wished that they did. And I would always rather ask, "What If I could?" rather than "What if I had?" "What if I could" is all about hope, whereas "What if I had" is usually about hurt.

Living by The Love Song Code means simply asking yourself, "What do I want? Which soundtrack will be the accompaniment of my life? Do I want to live and love the *What if I could?* life now or loathe the *What If I had?* one later?" The choice is yours. And you and your choices are the only things you have any real control over.

———————————————

So you've decided to go for it. To be bold. To be pro-active. To leave your imprint, in spite of any given circumstances or odds. To Risk Like a Love Song. Because you want your soundtrack to rock. You've said it out loud, written it down, and moved onward into action. And it's all going so great. Until... Life throws you another dissonant chord... Ouch—yet another un-welcomed Change that you didn't see coming. And this time, it's a doozy. You're told you're moving, and you didn't choose it. You're not getting a pay raise; it's a pay cut. You've lost your job. Squatters have stolen your property, etc. etc. What then? Well, then you must have more resolve then ever. Let's keep going and see if we can't just build something around a dissonant chord, shall we? Come on, just to see if it's possible. I'll show you my cards, I totally think it is.

THE KEY OF RESPONSE
RESPOND LIKE A JAZZ PLAYER

The Second Key we're going to play in/with is: The Key of Response.

I want you to Respond well.

I want you, as you Respond, to "settle or find a solution to a problem, dispute, or contentious matter."

What I call, **Respond Like a Jazz Player!**

Listen, people ask me all the time, "Robb, what about the changes that come, and they do come, that are completely out of our control, and wreak havoc on our plans? I know you know what I mean... I read the beginning of your book."

It's a great question, and the issue has never been better articulated than by that great, lucid and articulate voice, who often drops pearls of wisdom into humanity - Mike Tyson? - who once said, "Everyone's got a plan until they get punched in the mouth." I love that. Because it's just so true. Everyone has a plan. And then bam... It's like we need a plan for when things don't go according to plan. Ah ha... That's exactly what I love most about Jazz music.

Jazz music is difficult to define. Its range is so vast; it's like several music genres in one. Many of us have heard buzz words like "ragtime," "syncopation," and "swing." But fewer are those aware that Jazz is credited with the advent of the modern drum set and terms like "cool" and "hip." Great Jazz, at its best, is marked by spontaneity. When it's even better than that, it's just plain smooth.

The Origins of Jazz music are nothing short of fascinating...

The Birth of Jazz = Oppressed people, dealing with incredibly difficult circumstances, finding an outlet, a vehicle, and a voice for responding to the adversity in their lives. Taking things that would otherwise be negative and creating something entirely new and positive. Brilliant.

Now that Jazz is over a century old, its absolute hallmark, regardless of the era, is Improvisation. Yes, it's exactly what it sounds like - creating music as you go along - but always ensuring you make your way back to the root. You see, great Jazz is always created around the concept of a plan, a root, a key, a progression. Chaos would ensue if there were no plan. Improvisation works because everyone knows within what key they are grounded. There is an intent to Improv. There is an established root that is coupled with an exploratory outlook and a "throw whatever you will at me" mentality. The early pioneers of Jazz knew that becoming a great Improviser meant you were always more likely to land on your feet... In or out of a tune. So it's like chaos with a plan so that when the chaos of life comes, you can always get back to plan. A plan that, oddly enough, has usually been enhanced by the journey through the chaos.

The results of such mastery have unlocked chords, scales, and sounds that had never previously been charted or heard before in traditional music.

Seriously, I'm not sure anyone actually knows how many chords there are in the realm of music. And, honestly, I don't need to know... (It's not keeping me up at night or anything). But what I do know is that Jazz music is responsible for an overwhelming amount of them. New chords. New expressions. Birthed out of less-than-desirable circumstances. And I think we can all learn a lot from that.

When I lived in Las Vegas, I founded and ran a Community Service Organization.

Our team leased space in a building for the build out of a new community center. It was essentially a big box warehouse. An open canvas. A big rectangular space. With nothing in it save two small bathrooms. And based on our plans for the space, those rooms, in the condition that they were in, needed to come down.

The contractor informed us that if we could muster a volunteer crew, he would use us and oversee the demolition of the two rooms, saving us some much-needed cash on labor. So we went out and recruited about twenty volunteers, and we gathered them in the space. We informed them that our goal for the day was to tear down those two rooms. Sounded like fun. Demolition usually is.

So there we were with sledgehammers and various tools ripe for doing some serious damage.

Contractor said: "Just reduce it to a pile of debris and rubble."

Volunteer crew collectively: "Awesome!"

Awesome indeed. I remember the collective excitement over everyone "taking their shots," as it were. There were small, petite women (possibly with anger issues) saying things like, "You see that sheetrock? That sheetrock's name is Tim... And do you know what Tim did to me? And do you know what I'm gonna do to Tim?!" And with that, they would wield a sledgehammer that weighed nearly as much as they did, swing it with absolute brute force, and dismantle entire sheets of drywall with a single shot. I remember saying, "That is amazing, but I think you might want to talk with somebody though..."

Honestly, we all had a blast and within just two short hours we had completely demolished those two rooms. Just two hours. Two hours and there was not a single sign that those two rooms had ever existed with the exception of the dust we left in our wake.

Eventually, we turned things over to a professional labor force to begin construction. There is something interesting to take note of here. Even with the use of professionals at this point, it took a lot longer than two hours to create even a single bathroom to replace one of the two we had demolished. The logistical planning of pipe placement alone engulfs far more than 120 minutes. Not to mention the framing of what will become walls and a ceiling. The hanging, taping, plastering, and sanding of the sheetrock. Countertops, tile, sinks, stalls, and commodes. Everything from filament to fixtures to fans (for proper ventilation, of course - always necessary in a bathroom by the way).

The truth is, creation is always more difficult. Construction always brings a greater challenge. Always more effort. And, it should be noted, always more reward. Nothing worth doing or having comes without some kind of fight. Conversely, the unfortunate fact of the matter is, it's just so easy to deconstruct, and to tear things down. Anybody can do that. So most people do. And, if we're truly honest, there can be a cheap thrill in it. An opportunity to take out our aggression, anger, and frustrations for all those times when things didn't or don't go our way.

When life deals out circumstances that are less than desirable, it is often too easy for a human to descend into negativity and excuse it away, calling it maturity. You know how this goes, "I used to be (insert any positive thought here)... when I was young. But then I grew up and became more realistic." That's not maturity. It's just cynicism, and being jaded isn't a virtue. When life brings the adversity of an un-welcomed Change, (and it WILL bring this adversity sooner or later), too many people opt for this path of least resistance and become deconstructionists of the highest order. I hear this type of talk all the time, and it really drives me nuts!

What would happen though, if, even when faced with a challenge, in the middle of an un-welcomed Change, you chose to create rather than tear down? What if, instead, you chose to become a Constructionist rather than a Deconstructionist? Well, you might just make great Jazz.

The Improvisational stylings of Jazz are based on what is known as Call and Response. A Call is sung or played by the Band Leader, and then the other instrumentalists must quickly adapt and respond with a creation of their own that seeks to create greatness. So... Life calls out and throws you a dissonant chord, how do you respond? Like a jazz player trying to explore new territory or like a deconstructionist that brings sweet music to a grinding halt?

Again, before moving on, consider the following questions and do a little self-assessment:
- There is a change of procedure, a policy at work. Some people spew negativity before even considering its benefits. Others look into its potential and give it a fair shake before offering a critique. Which best describes you?

- Someone (not named you) in the office has a new (really good) idea. It will change things. Some people deconstruct and tear it down. But some see it as a starting point, help to make it better, and ultimately achievable for the sake of the greater good. Which one is a better match for you?

- Are you seeking to improve workflow and productivity in the company? Improve the sales pipeline? etc. Some people Innovate. Others complain. Who do you want to be?

- Do you support your friends/family through difficulty and help them find a way to something positive? Because some people don't, and make it easier for them to descend into cynicism.

- Do you celebrate and champion friends/colleagues/peers/and family when something great happens to them? Because some people deconstruct, feeling a sense of envy, as they wonder why others should be the recipients of such good fortune while secretly they wallow in their bitterness.

What if the adversity of an un-welcomed Change is actually a gift to you? And what if it could become a part of your path for the purpose of your growth and your benefit? And what if it's moved you out of your-box-of-comfort? And what if that was a great thing, because now, and only now, you can actually think outside-of-the-box?

What if it meant that you were on the brink of opening up new chords, scales, and sounds... Incorporating them into your life and your dealings in a way that you would never have thought possible otherwise? Ah, yes... The "What if I could?" life. Here it comes.

robboverholt

AN IMPROV PLAN
FOR WHEN THINGS DON'T GO ACCORDING TO PLAN

Ok, here's where we get really practical. Let's call this "out-of-the-box" thinking, Improv Planning... A plan for when things don't go according to plan. Choosing to create and break new ground rather than thinking "This sucks, so we stay stuck," is but one thing we learn from Jazz. But let's look just a little deeper into some basic Improv theories and principles that can help anyone continue to orchestrate, even in the midst of an un-welcomed Change.

In Improv, performers are presented with new data and everything is changing at a rapid pace. Literally, they are faced with what are called "problems" that they must learn to incorporate into their performance. They must interact with these "challenges." They cannot ignore them... That is simply not an option. There is no time to resist or debate; they must respond. That's a HUGE concept for the rest of us. And it gives us some amazing insights that we can all incorporate into our lives, regardless of our current circumstances.

So let's look into how we can begin to take on and overcome an un-welcomed Change and the challenges that it often brings.

First Step:
Objective - **Make Fun of the Problem**
Outcome - **Paralyzation to Potential**

One of the quintessential elements of Improv is to "make fun of the problem." It doesn't necessarily make the problem more fun, but it does make it more manageable as we reassume our rightful position over the challenge instead of the challenge looming over and dictating terms to us.

In, perhaps, Jazz music's greatest derivative, the Blues, a good anecdote often became a great antidote for the frustrations of life's greatest challenges. This type of thinking allowed me to channel my inner BB King and produce a little ditty containing a lyric that goes something like this:

"I bought her a brand new car
She said she wanted a truck
Made her a real fancy dinner
Thought I might start to have better luck
Bought her a brand new house
And she called it a shack
Purchased a vacation for two
She took my brother,
And they haven't come back...
She's my lady,

At least she was till lately,
Now she's my brother's lady and she left me
the blues..."

> *- My Lady Took Everything , but Left Me*
> *the Blues, (and I Got the Better End of*
> *the Deal)* - by Robb Overholt

The problem, the challenge, in the tune is not a lady at all. The lady is a metaphor. The real character is the oppressor, be it a person, a circumstance, or a situation, it doesn't matter. In this case, the character literally represents "the loss of my dream job." Seriously, I wrote this and used it as a reminder that the only thing I could control was my response. I couldn't control the conditions and loss of the "dream job" that I pursued for so long any more than I could a fickle filly that's hell-bent on betrayal. And even though I was convinced that she was the one for me, it turns out that there *are* other fish in the sea, and now I'm better off without her. I jest, and that's the point. Take the "challenge," the "change" that is out of your control and poke fun at it. Give it a relatable identify and then write a new script for that identity, so you can begin to control your response, and its outcome, rather than it controlling you.

You see, most of us make a deity out of our problems and concerns, don't we? They engulf and hover over us and demand the majority of our attention. We think we need the problem's permission to move forward. We think the problem has all the authority and say in what happens next. It's not true. And by making fun of the problem, we bring it back down to a manageable level. We reassume our rightful position over "it" rather than "it" looming over and dictating terms to us. It's true; a good anecdote does make for a great antidote.

I did some follow-up with a group I led through this teaching. Based on this step, a Senior Leader had turned the elements of the problems, brought on by an un-welcomed Change, into cartoon characters. He then, along with his co-workers, wrote a quick story about what happens to these characters that mimicked the fate of Wile E. Coyote (whose schemes always backfired to his own detriment). He announced, "We determined that no matter how hard the new challenges (brought on by a change) tried to foil our plans, it was the change's plans that would be foiled." The team took note that this was an immense help to them in overcoming the paralyzation that the problem(s) had created. Incredible. He and his colleagues had now reassumed authority in their circumstances and moved forward with a new confidence and broke new ground in spite of the obstacles that they faced.

You may be thinking, "That's great, but I'm not that creative." I assure you that you are. Regardless, *don't do this alone*. The chances that you, on your own, can find any humor during a challenging trial, are diminished. Invite others in, asking them to help you find the levity in the midst of the difficulty.

A century ago, Sigmund Freud pointed out that humor offers a healthy means of coping with life stress. Long before that, an ancient proverb told us "A cheerful heart is good medicine, but a crushed spirit dries up the bones." It's true, even in the direst situations. For example, you can often hear laughter at a funeral wake as people share stories in the midst of grief that they are just beginning to process. If humor can work in the most extreme cases, certainly it can trickle down to other issues and milder traumas that we experience in our lives. It can and it does. Humor brings with it, hope.

The point is, make fun of the problem, before the problem makes someone or something else out of you. Find a way to tell the challenge what it is instead of it telling you what you are. Don't start by being a prisoner to it or ignoring it. Don't try to give it a quick-fix and eliminate it either. As hard as it may be to believe, this un-welcomed Change may eventually be of benefit to you, so start by reframing it.

Once you've completed this step, you can now interact with the change, rather than ignore or be submissive to it, in much the same way you do with the rest of your intentions. In doing so, it's no longer an obstacle to your desired outcome; it is a part of the path towards your desired outcome. It is there for a reason. And in many cases, based on my experience, if you master this type of behavior, it usually enhances your desired outcome rather than destroying it.

You're now ready for the next great element in a good Improv Plan...

Second Step:
Objective - **Learn to Play by Ear**
Outcome - **Pity to Possibility**

Now that the problems aren't so daunting, great Improv planners begin to relax as they start to get in tune and take cues from the challenges in the environment around them. They now become great listeners. In a more at-ease state, they begin picking up nuances that others might easily brush past due to their stress.

Learning to Play by Ear is not some utopian, laid back mush... "Uh, I'll just take it as it comes, huh-huh." No way. It's a skill that requires training. So how do we train our ears as great listeners while we learn from the challenges in our environment? It's quite simple: Start asking questions, and then listen for and to the responses.

The good news is, questioning things is already quite natural for us to do when faced with the stress of an un-welcomed Change. The not-so-good news is, we are often asking the wrong questions. In fact, more often than not, we ask questions, with a focus on pity, and we start with "Why" or "Who."

For example:
"Why is this happening to me?"
- or -
"Who is responsible for this?"

In this state of mind, we are usually too anxious to find someone/something to blame as we have already surmised that we didn't do anything to deserve this hardship. If we can't find a responsible party, we will often eventually blame God or the Universe (vantage point pending). Someone is going to take the fall. Let me be clear: This progression of thought is a dangerous road to bitterness that is not worth its travel expenses.

Never ask these *why* and *who* "pity" questions and categorically reject this line of thinking as soon as possible. It's unproductive. The honest, brutal truth is, you will likely never know or get satisfactory answers to these kinds of questions. Even if you should get answers, it is often only with the benefit of hindsight, when you can look back and see the circumstances from a better vantage point. You must first get through the challenge that is at hand.

So instead, start asking, "possibility" questions:

"What" i.e.
- "What do I have here?"
- "What is at my disposal?"
- "I know what this looks like, but... What could it actually be?"

Or, better still…
- "What could this become?"

And perhaps, most importantly:
- "What am I going to do about it?"

More great questions:

"How" i.e.
- "How do I engage with this?"
- "How do I move forward?"
- "How do I incorporate it into my current path and plans?"

The reason is simple… When dealing with a hurdle, any un-welcomed Change, we should always look first for awareness, not analysis. In Improvisation, performers don't have time to ask, "Why did they play the note/melody like that?" or "Who does it that way?" And when you face an un-welcomed Change and the problems that it creates, you don't either. You simply have time to respond and create. The answer to "why" and "who" may or may not come later, but right now you have to get through the challenge.

Never forget, Improvisation is collaborative in its very nature. *You shouldn't try it alone*, and it always happens best when it is Team/Communally based. There is a greater perspective for a greater result. So, please, *DON'T ask these "pity" questions in isolation*, but *DO ask "possibility" questions in community.* Take the time to have brainstorming sessions as a team in small groups, or even large groups. If it's a personal matter, go to the people you trust, who give you wisdom. Ask the right questions of them, listen intently, and record your results. Now, you can craft a new, and quite possibly improved, plan utilizing the aforementioned results. It's that simple!

I spoke with a well-established CEO after an event who told me how much she could relate to the insights from this section in my material. She told me her employees spend so much time and energy asking "Why" when they have to cope with an issue caused by a work-related, (or any other type of), change. She too had noticed that they typically look for "Who" to blame for their stress. She said, "I tell them, 'When it gets to my desk, I don't care about "Why" or about "Who." Blame it on me if you must. I just want to know "What" we're going to do about it and "How" we're going to get it done.'" Please know that most good leaders, like her, are on the look-out for problem solvers, who will take ownership in creating optimum outcomes in spite of difficulties.

That makes for a great segue to our final step...

Third Step:
Objective - **Remember to Breathe**
Outcome - **Preservation to Production**

Many of the great jazz legends are known for their prowess on the trumpet. Think Louis Armstrong, Miles Davis, and Dizzy Gillespie. They are famous for their breathing techniques. And then there's the saxophone. Don't even get me started. The greats master something called "circular breathing." They are trained and able to inhale through their nose, store air in their cheeks, and exhale through their mouths, simultaneously. Giving them the ability to bring in air and evacuate it at the same time. In doing so, they can produce a sustained tone, without interruptions. This incredible discipline is *not* natural. It is something that must be learned and diligently mastered.

As we face uncertainty, it is of the utmost importance that we remember and master our most basic rhythm, our breathing. Let's try a little exercise here...

When dealing with the challenges of an un-welcomed Change:

Some people go into a perpetual state of self-preservation and find it difficult to recover. They may even simply grab everything they can and cling to it, propelled by fear. However, the only movement being created is a retreat towards what they think is safety. They will attempt to save or store everything they can. As a result, now life is just happening *to* them, rather than them making life happen. They are like people who breathe in constantly without ever exhaling. Taking in air but never letting it go. Let's experiment with that and see what it feels like for a moment, shall we? Seriously, give it a shot. Go ahead and take a deep breath in, but don't exhale. Take another breath in, but don't let it go. Keep doing this repeatedly for as long as you can. I'll wait. It won't be long.

How did that work out? Not so great, huh? It's as if the lungs are just going to explode. They need a release. And so do you.

Let's consider another common response from the other side of the spectrum:

For others, preservation finds them simply going through the motions, trying to ignore the obvious problems and issues created by an un-welcomed Change. Staying busy, they are burning out faster than a candle lit from both ends. They continue doing things at manic rates without any regard for focusing, in order that they might learn from and master the challenge. They refuse to accept this "change" and are trying to convince themselves that if they ignore it, it will simply go away. They can be likened to someone who breathes out constantly without ever inhaling. Let's give that a shot as well. Go ahead and evacuate a deep breath from your lungs, but don't inhale more oxygen. Exhale again without taking in any air. Continue for as long as you are able.

Well? This time it's as if the lungs are going to implode, right? And either way, this behavior will not sustain you, and it will eventually lead to a lack of productivity and death.

In order to survive in the face of adversity, not to mention, thrive, we must breathe in and breathe out. First, literally... If you are going through a difficult challenge even now, take a deep breath and then evacuate that breath as you exhale. It's amazing how good that can feel. Know this: You will survive, and this too will pass. It will. Of equal, if not more, value to us though, this is an important metaphor in order for you to thrive. Breathe in and out. Simultaneously, when possible.

Breathe in and absorb it. Accept it. Recognize that these are *your* circumstances, no one else's, and you have a role and responsibility in them. You are *not* a victim. Adamantly refuse to see yourself as one. Everyone has difficulties in life, and no one gets through unscathed. Pay more attention than ever and take note of everything in your environment. Own your ability to choose now how you will move forward, because you and your choices are the only things you have any real control over. Listen and learn from what this change and its challenges will teach you, and they are likely to teach you much.

Meanwhile, continue breathing out. Keep on keeping on. Take what you are learning, and apply it to action. Late eighteenth-century German writer, Johann Wolfgang von Goethe observed, "Knowing is not enough; we must apply. Willing is not enough; we must do." And I couldn't agree more. Go. Intently move forward, creating in motion, exhaling your influence and energy into the world as you push on with a renewed plan towards your desired outcomes. Resolve to carry on.

Assume ownership and take action, simultaneously, when possible. Do this for a more sustained tone physically, mentally, emotionally, and spiritually. We can't assume that this kind of behavior will simply emerge. It will not happen automatically. The opposite is true. This metaphoric circular breathing is not any more natural than the physical act. It's a discipline. Honestly, it's not normal to maintain a sustained tone when facing the difficulties that an un-welcomed Change can bring. It can be done, but it is something that must be learned and diligently mastered. We must constantly nurture this type of responsiveness through a variety of ongoing challenges that will eventually lead to both our personal and professional development. Strategically, we should seek to master this type of behavior as soon as possible, so it's a natural discipline to fall back on when life's difficult challenges come our way. So let's get started right now.

Take the "Breathing 101" Challenge:

Commit to learning at least one new, positive, thing each week for one month (Breathe in)... And immediately apply it to your life (Breathe out). Breathe in and learn from others who may be a tad further along in life's journey. Or from someone who has a particular area of expertise in your field. Or maybe even someone who is knowledgeable in a subject or hobby of personal interest. Start lessons. Take a class. Get a mentor. Then, immediately, incorporate these learnings (whatever they are) into your life and begin to breathe out your influence into the world. Don't hold onto the newfound learnings, utilize them. Do this for one month and see if it does not begin to produce immediate results in your life.

If you don't know where to start, I'm going to help you. I've asked four of my contemporaries to come up with a unique teaching to share with and challenge you. Each one of them has a distinct brilliance, and they are quite accomplished in their own right. They have all agreed to help because that is their nature. To opt in and get started now, simply go to my website at www.robboverholt.com/#/breathing-101 and click yes on the "Breathing 101" challenge form. That's it. Just let me know, and I will email you one of these challenges each Monday morning. So that's one teaching a week, from a different perspective, for a month. You will be off to an incredible start; I assure you. After the month is over, sustain this new practice. You will be equipped to orchestrate your desired outcomes, regardless of what's being thrown at you. By voluntarily choosing to be challenged anew on a weekly basis, you will be far better suited to take on any challenge that comes, whether you volunteered for it or not. At that moment, you will think, "I do this all the time. This challenge will be no different."

Rather than behaving with a bad reflex to deconstruct and then thinking later, "I could have handled that better..." You are now training yourself to be constructive.

In science, business, government, music, marriage, friendship, you name it... The ability to create in motion, with our hands open to the possibilities, and to think on our feet (while they are moving), is a valued skill. A skill that is often associated with leadership, innovation, and success.

By way of review, you can now:

1. Move from paralyzation to potential as you **make fun of the problem...** Reframing it so that you are now telling it what it is rather than it telling you who you are.

2. Go from pity to possibility as you **learn to play by ear,** asking the right questions, learning in community with those you are working with or those that you trust.

3. Take a journey from preservation to productivity as you begin to **breathe in** the circumstances and your newfound role and responsibility in them. You now accept and assume ownership, applying your learnings simultaneously, creating on your feet as you **breathe out.** Practice this discipline regularly for a more sustained tone.

This strategy will work, and you will be amazed at the results. "Risk" is boldly and proactively pushing past the fear of our circumstances or odds for the desired result of creating positive change. Great "Response" with an Improv Plan is creating through negative circumstances for the very same thing. It puts the impending change back in our court. Now it's no longer something that has happened to us, but something that we are using to make our desired outcomes happen. The difference and the results are staggering.

EMBRACE THE TENSION?

Let's be frank, change, be it a positive change that we are trying to create or the un-welcomed kind that we do not author, will bring tension into our lives. This life is already fraught with adversity and challenges that ultimately bring us tension. Furthermore, it's been my experience that humans don't tend to like tension. Most of us spend a great deal of our time trying to reduce or eliminate tension. We will avoid conflicts, settle for mediocrity as an existence, and, even times, accept insufferable outcomes. All the while convincing ourselves that we did the right thing because we were spared the tension. The irony here is such behavior will only inevitably cause the tension to increase to unhealthy and often harsher outcomes.

But what if the tension is not a problem to solve, but a necessary part of our lives that we must learn to orchestrate as well? Maybe alleviating it is not the right goal and tension exists for a reason and can be good too. Yes, I meant to express that perhaps tension has a purpose and can, at times, be a positive thing. That would, of course, mean that perhaps we need to and should embrace the tension.

I couldn't blame you for being slightly puzzled by this perspective. You may even be thinking, "I was with you, Robb. Until you started that crazy talk about embracing tension. I go to the spa to release tension." Or, "Tension is the reason I'm nestled up to a bar after hours." Or, "Tension is why I play Golf." Or, "Golf is the reason I have tension."

Honestly, I know. I do. You would be well within the realm of reason to demand some proof for such a point of view. And the only thing I have to offer is the Guitar. Any stringed instrument would do, but the guitar is the one with which I am most familiar. I would like to enter it here as Exhibit A.

A basic acoustic guitar has six strings, four of which are wound... Tight. Did you know that? Do you know anybody like that, wound tight? If you don't, it's probably you. The other two strings are very thin in comparison and are much more delicate and quite brittle in their disposition. Again, sound like anyone you know? These wound-tight strings and their more fragile counterparts are inserted into what is called a bridge. They are then run across a fret board and saddled into a small strip of bone commonly called a nut. Next, they are taken through what are referred to as machine heads or tuning pegs. These heads are then turned, cranking up gears within them that begin to apply to these wound-tight and brittle strings... You guessed it... Tension.

The goal, of course, is the right amount of tension. But certainly not, no tension at all. Or, even too little tension for that matter. That just produces the blah sound of a mundane and lackluster existence. Of course, the goal is not too much tension either. That s-t-r-e-t-c-h-e-s the strings far beyond their limits, and that doesn't feel good at all and eventually causes one or more to snap and break.

It's not hard to see where I'm going here. The obvious goal is a balanced tension, but a real tension all the same. Managed - not alone, mind you, but in the company of others balancing and managing the tension as well.

What if, for the sake of metaphor, the strings weren't strings at all, but were people? Like you and like me. And what if we got the tension in balance, with others who were holding this tension in balance?

What if Marketing and Accounting were to exist in balanced tension together?
- Employer and Employee?
- Management and Labor?
- Producer and Consumer?
- President and Congress?
- School and Student?
- Husband and Wife?
- Partner and Partner?
- Parent and Child?
- You name it…

Seriously, think of all the possibilities.

What if strings were like team members? Or a family? A community? A company? etc. Balancing and navigating the tension so much so that when pressure started to be applied to them… Yes, pressure now applied to tension (think fingers on the fret board here), so that the orchestration of new notes and sounds are now being produced. And when pressure finds its way to multiple "strings" simultaneously, new chords can even be heard. Of course, these new sounds can only be created when a "string" is picked, or when "strings" are rattled as they are strummed abrasively. So, now you have tension, pressure, and picking/rattling. All for the purpose of creating a beautiful composition. Again, I ask, what if all these things meant that we might open up new chords and sounds and incorporate them into our lives and our dealings in a way that we would never have thought possible otherwise? What might be possible then?

Go to the playground of your imagination and swing on the monkey bars there for just a moment... Imagine the possibilities. Ok, back to reality. No, really... Snap out of it. There is much to get done. And it's time to get started.

> "You're off to great places; today is
> your day. Your mountain is waiting,
> So... Get on your way!" - Dr. Seuss

My work here is just about complete. But, before I finish, let me just remind you that, in spite of the fact that change can be difficult, sometimes it comes along at the perfect time in our lives. Almost as if it knew that things were starting to feel predictable and stale. When this type of thing happens, it can delight us in the same manner as a song that delivers a brilliant change of key as it makes its way to the coda. I'm thinking of a classic example of that type of song now. It is, perhaps, one of the best key changes I've ever heard in the annals of pop culture. It's housed in a tune that made a kid from Jersey, calling himself Jon Bon Jovi, a household name, even though he changed it from the name he grew up with in his household.

The tune, of which I now write, remains to be regularly cited as "the most sung along to song" by folks that create such lists. It's about a young couple *fighting to hold on to each other in spite of everything being thrown at them. His name is Tommy, and he's hit hard times with the Union on strike and little work to be found. Gina, his girl, waits tables at the diner day in and day out, bringing home precious little, but some much-needed pay. Taking each other's hands, they are emboldened* to Risk Like a

Love Song, and *it nearly appears too overwhelming.* But as the story unfolds*, it happens... The key change. Woah, Oh! They are off and running,* ready to Respond Like Jazz Players. Sure, it might seem silly. And, on the surface, we may even make fun of them at times. But underneath it all, we all know that we really admire their courage.

You've been equipped with some knowledge here, so you're *halfway there* as well. But remember, knowing is not enough.

Will you apply it? Will you *give it a shot?*

EPILOGUE

There is a state park in the Mojave Desert of Southern Nevada called The Valley of Fire. The kind of place where car commercials are filmed with warnings like: "Professional Driver on a Closed Course." Lest we think we might ever dare to drive in such a fashion. During a visit with my family, we took in the stunning beauty of the red sandstone formations and stood amidst the shifting sand dunes. As we were exploring, we happened upon some cave drawings. We would discover that these petroglyphs were some 3,000 years old.

Sketches and diagrams on rock formations that told stories. Drawings of a primitive people showing how they lived, worked, danced, and played. They had found a way to leave their mark.

In addition, there were artifacts of crude musical instruments there too... Originally made of wood and animal skins and the like. It was sobering to take in the stories and imagine the soundtracks of these native people, whoever they were. At the risk of seeming dramatic, it was like the voices of the dead were calling out to those of us who are still here. It was as if they were saying, "We had a purpose for being here. So don't waste yours."

And it occurred to me that if you were to find a primitive civilization today buried deep in the jungle or alone on a remote island... A tribe or a people who knew nothing of modern civilization, and had not been touched by the Digital Age with its Information Superhighway. No one outside of their tribe could mutter or understand a word of their dialect... A complete language barrier. Still living in this primitive state, there would be nothing at all to connect them to us ------- except, two things of course... Stories and Soundtracks.

That is why I choose to communicate using these most powerful mediums. As a storyteller who can incorporate a little bit of soundtrack to assist, I use these universal languages to present universal principles that never change. I do this in order to help us all orchestrate leaving our imprint into a world, a culture, and a marketplace where change is constant.

You know as I think back to our trip that day in the desert, it's as if all people, throughout all time have inherently desired to share their story. They, too, have known that they could use a good tune to help them do it. Throughout history and the ages, people have always found a way to leave their mark. So let's agree that we should be intentional about leaving one too. I'm Robb Overholt, and I would love to work with you and/or your organization to help you do just that... To Create and

Orchestrate Your Desired Outcomes in a
world and a marketplace that is in a
constant state of flux.

ABOUT THE AUTHOR

Robb Overholt is The Change Orchestrator. His primary goal and sincere passion is to empower you to become a Change Conductor of your own. A captivating motivational speaker and an innovative thought leader, Robb's universal and versatile message is a perfect fit for anyone in any organization. Hailing from Austin, TX, Robb draws from his life experience as a business owner, adventurer, musician, activist, philanthropist, husband, and father to deliver presentations that are both memorable and motivational.

For more information, go to www.robboverholt.com or email info@robboverholt.com.

Made in the USA
Charleston, SC
13 November 2015